Gloria in excelsis Deo

from the Mass Proper

5

6

God be in my head

Horae B. V. M. (Sarum) 1514

Alexander L'Estrange

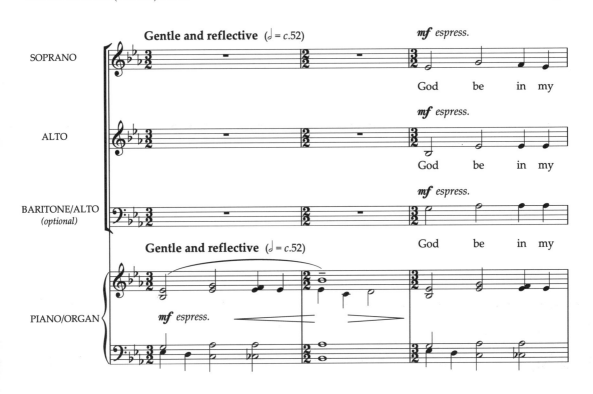

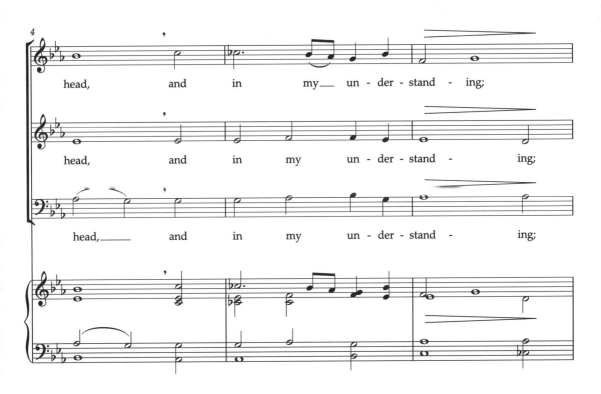

8

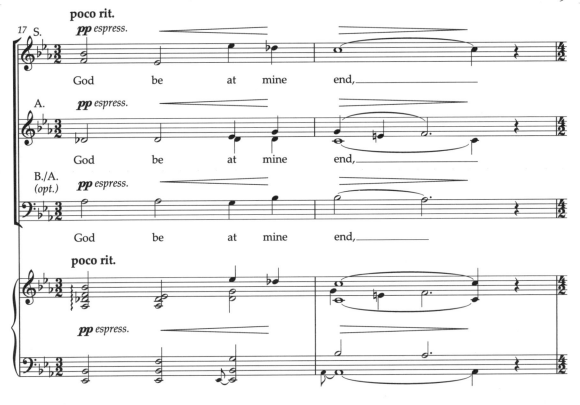

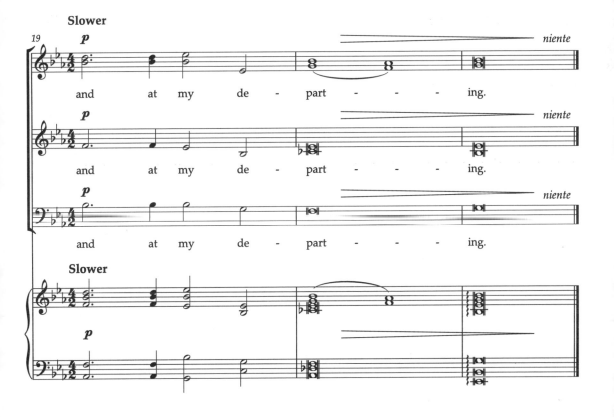

Ave verum corpus

14th-century Eucharistic Hymn

Wolfgang Amadeus Mozart
arr. Alexander L'Estrange

Zadok the Priest

(from *Zadok the Priest: Coronation Anthem*)

after 1 Kings 1: 39–40

George Frideric Handel
arr. Ben Parry

14

Ave Maria

Marian antiphon

Franz Schubert
arr. Ben Parry

18

Jubilate

Psalm 100

Ben Parry

24

27

Scotland, December 2006

Panis Angelicus

St Thomas Aquinas
(1225–74)

César Franck
arr. Ben Parry

con Ped.

The Lord is my Shepherd

(theme from *The Vicar of Dibley*)

from Psalm 23

Howard Goodall

Amazing Grace

John Newton

Traditional
arr. Alexander L'Estrange

38

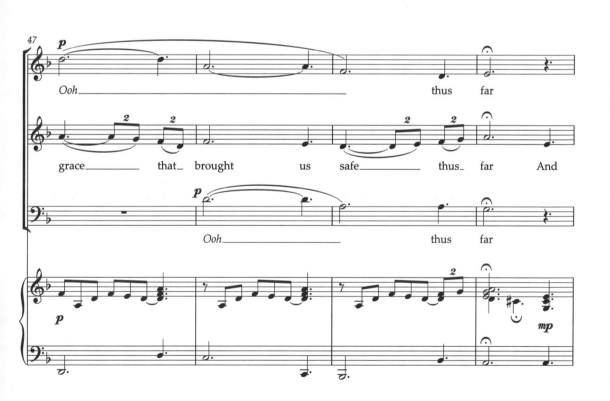

40

grace will lead us home. The

poco rit.

Moving on again (♩. = 84)

Lord has pro - mised good to me, His

Moving on again (♩. = 84)

word my hope se - cures He

'Hallelujah' Chorus
(from *Messiah*)

from Revelation

George Frideric Handel
arr. Ben Parry

44

46

Music for Special Occasions

Music for Special Occasions brings together 10 sacred choral works in one volume, carefully selected to cater for a wide variety of performance contexts – whether joyful, reflective or commemorative. Practically and flexibly arranged for soprano and alto, with an optional third part of limited range for baritone or low alto, this unique collection of best-loved classics and new pieces is a must-have resource for all school, community and church choirs.

Gloria in excelsis Deo · *Antonio Vivaldi*

God be in my head · *Alexander L'Estrange*

Ave verum corpus · *Wolfgang Amadeus Mozart*

Zadok the Priest · *George Frideric Handel*

Ave Maria · *Franz Schubert*

Jubilate · *Ben Parry*

Panis Angelicus · *César Franck*

The Lord is my Shepherd/Psalm 23 · *Howard Goodall*

Amazing Grace · *Traditional*

Hallelujah Chorus · *George Frideric Handel*

Also available:

Music for Special Occasions
10 secular choral arrangements

My love is like a red, red rose · *Traditional*
Ombra mai fu · *George Frideric Handel*
Bridal March · *Richard Wagner*
Londonderry Air · *Traditional*
She walks in beauty · *Alexander L'Estrange*
Ode to Joy · *Ludwig van Beethoven*
You'll never walk alone · *Rodgers & Hammerstein*
Congratulations · *Cliff Richard*
Circle of Life (with Nants' Ingonyama) · *Elton John*
Auld Lang Syne · *Traditional*

ISBN10:   0-571-52496-6
EAN13:   978-0-571-52496-9

FABER *ff* MUSIC
fabermusic.com

9 780571 524969 >